DEMCO

EXTRAORDINARY STORIES BEHIND

The INVENTION
of
ORDINARY THINGS

DON L. WULFFSON
Illustrated by
ROY DOTY

LOTHROP, LEE & SHEPARD BOOKS
New York

Text copyright © 1981 by Don L. Wulffson
Illustrations copyright © 1981 by Roy Doty

Library of Congress Cataloging in Publication Data

Wulffson, Don L
    The invention of ordinary things.

    SUMMARY: Traces the origin or invention of 28 common, everyday items, such as shopping carts, jigsaw puzzles, frozen foods, zippers, safety pins, vacuum cleaners, and rubber bands.
    1. Inventions—History—Juvenile literature. [1. Inventions—History] I. Doty, Roy, (date) II. Title.
T15.W84   608   80–17498
ISBN 0–688–41978–X   ISBN 0–688–51978–4 (lib. bdg.)

Contents

The Shopping Cart

Today there are twenty to twenty-five million shopping carts rolling around the world. In fact, the shopping cart is presently the most often used item on four wheels, second only to the automobile.

Indeed, almost everybody in America will spend a part of his or her life behind a shopping cart. They will, in a lifetime, push the chrome-plated contraptions many miles. But few will know—or even think to ask—who it was that invented them.

Mr. Sylvan N. Goldman of Oklahoma City invented the shopping cart in 1937. Mr. Goldman's invention did not make him famous. It did, however, make him *very* rich.

When Goldman invented the cart he was in the supermarket business. Every day he would see shoppers lugging groceries around in baskets that they had to carry.

One day Goldman suddenly had the idea of putting baskets on wheels. The wheeled baskets would make shopping much easier for his customers. And by lightening their chore, he would attract their business.

Pondering the idea, Goldman walked into his office and sat down on a folding chair. Looking down at the chair, Goldman had another idea. The carts, he realized, should be made so they could be folded up. This would make it easier to store them when not in use.

NEW!
SHOPPING
CARTS

On June 4, 1937, Goldman's first batch of carts was ready for use in his market. He was terribly excited on the morning of that day as customers began arriving. He couldn't wait to see them using his invention.

But Goldman was disappointed. Most shoppers gave the carts a long look, but hardly anybody would give them a try.

After a while, Goldman decided to ask customers why they weren't using his carts. "Don't you think this arm is strong enough to carry a shopping basket?" one offended shopper replied.

Day after day, the same thing happened. People wouldn't use the carts. They preferred a basket on the arm to a basket on wheels.

But Goldman wasn't beaten yet. He knew his carts would be a great success if only he could persuade people to give them a try. To this end, Goldman tried something that was both very clever and very funny. Believe it or not, he hired a group of people to push carts around his market and pretend they were shopping! Seeing this, the real customers gradually began copying the phony customers.

As Goldman had hoped, the carts were soon attracting larger and larger numbers of customers to his market. But not only did more people come—those who came bought more. With larger, easier-to-handle baskets, customers unconsciously bought a greater number of items than before.

Today's shopping carts are five times larger than Gold-man's original model. Perhaps that's one reason Americans today spend more than five times as much money on food each year as they did before 1937—before the coming of the shopping cart.

Shoes

Human beings have been on earth for about two million years, and most of that time they have been walking around in their bare feet. No one knows exactly when, but somewhere along the line someone had the bright idea of making shoes. The first of these were probably leaves or animal skins wrapped around the feet; then came sandals, another invention of a now nameless person.

Next came boots, which at first were worn only by hunters, noblemen, or soldiers going into battle. Peasants either wore wooden clogs or went barefoot.

Early boots had neither soles nor heels, with the result that there were a lot of cold, wet feet when the weather turned bad. For this reason, during the fifteenth century people began strapping wooden blocks to their boots on days when it snowed or rained. Soon the platform and the boot were combined, creating the forerunner to modern footwear—shoes with soles and heels.

Early footgear was completely straight—there was no effort on the part of craftsmen to differentiate between the left foot and the right. For the soldiers of Rome, the kings and queens of the Middle Ages, and the early American colonists there was no such thing as a left shoe and a right shoe: shoes were identical and interchangeable. Not until around 1850 did shoes shaped differently for each foot come into being.

11

Over the centuries there have been some very strange fads and fashions where footwear is concerned. For example, in fifteenth-century England people took to wearing shoes with long, pointed ends. In time, the shoes got so long that the ends had to be attached to the wearer's knees! To put a stop to all this nonsense, the government passed a law forbidding the wearing of excessively long shoes. This brought the fad to an abrupt halt, at the same time generating another, even stranger fad—the wearing of short, flat, extra-wide shoes!

One fad that has known sporadic popularity throughout history is the wearing of high heels. Interestingly, it was a man rather than a woman who first used them. King Louis XIV of France, embarrassed by the fact that he was shorter than almost everybody else, ordered the royal cobbler to make him a pair of platform shoes with super-high heels.

Influenced by the example of the petite king, both men and women began experimenting with bigger, higher heels. In time, men grew tired of the fashion and abandoned it; women, on the other hand, perpetuated the fashion, pursuing it to outrageous extremes. In fact, by the end of the seventeenth century women were wearing shoes with heels so high that they couldn't even walk in them. To keep from falling down, ladies took to hiring servants to lean on whenever it was necessary to get from one place to another!

Truly, some of these footwear fads of the past were incredibly funny—almost as funny as some of the fads of today. Witness, for example, silver lamé shoes with stacked heels for men, platform shoes with eight-inch soles for women, and Donald Duck slippers for kids.

But all of this is nothing when compared to some custom-made shoes recently created by an American manufacturer. The heels of the shoes were made of clear, hollowed-out plastic, and could be filled with water and live goldfish—turning the wearer, in effect, into a walking aquarium!

Jigsaw Puzzles

Today's jigsaw puzzles are intended as entertainment—as a pleasant, challenging way to pass the time. Surprisingly, however, the very first jigsaw puzzle was designed as a teaching device, not an entertainment.

"For the purpose of teaching geography," John Spilsbury, an Englishman, created the first-ever jigsaw puzzle in the year 1767. Made of wood and hand-painted, the puzzle was a map of England and Wales; each county made up a separate piece.

Spilsbury created about thirty different map puzzles, all of which he sold commercially "as a means whereby children may learn of geography." In 1782 he gave up his puzzle business and became an art teacher at an English school.

Before the end of the eighteenth century, pictorial jig-saw puzzles began to appear. One of the earliest shows a farm girl offering a jug of fresh milk to a young man.

As with Spilsbury's map puzzles, the pieces in these early pictorial puzzles were not interlocking. Not until the invention of power tools more than a century later did jigsaw puzzles with fully interlocking pieces make their appearance.

Today there are jigsaw puzzles of every size, shape and design imaginable. There are puzzles that are completely blank, and puzzles can be custom-made of a picture of your-self or a friend or relative. There are tiny puzzles and there are giant, room-size puzzles, the largest of which measures almost 20 feet by 16 feet and contains 40,000 pieces.

Breakfast Cereal

The story behind the invention of breakfast cereal is an extremely strange one. Believe it or not, this ordinary, mundane product came into being as a result of a religious vision!

It all started with an American woman by the name of Ellen White. Miss White, it seems, was passionately religious. Not infrequently, she had strangely vivid dreams—dreams in which she saw and spoke to figures from the Bible.

One night she dreamed that she met God himself. He told her that no one should use tobacco, eat meat, or drink coffee, tea, or liquor.

Believing she had a divine mission to carry out, Miss White established the Health Reform Institute at Battle Creek, Michigan. One member of the institute was Charles Post. Post devised a coffee substitute, a cereal beverage which he called "Postum." He also invented a dry breakfast food. At first it was called "Elijah's Manna," but the name didn't go over very well with the public, so it was changed to "Grape-Nuts."

Another member of the Institute was a surgeon by the name of Dr. John Harvey Kellogg. Chiefly for the benefit of a patient who had broken her false teeth, Dr. Kellogg devised a breakfast cereal he called "Corn Flakes."

Within a few years, Americans everywhere were adopting the custom of having a quick bowl of cold cereal for breakfast. As for Mr. Post and Mr. Kellogg, both became very wealthy. And Miss White, who had started it all, continued working at her Institute by day—and having strange dreams and visions by night.

Playing Cards

Playing cards were invented by the Chinese over a thousand years ago. Some of the cards had dots on them, and were nothing more than paper dice. Other cards had pictures on them—and were designed to look like packs of paper money.

Playing cards reached Europe during the thirteenth century, about three hundred years after their invention by the Chinese. In Europe, the cards were called "Tarots." At first they were used for fortune-telling, not for playing games.

Early Chinese decks contained thirty cards; European tarot decks contained seventy-four. When people in Europe began using the tarots for gambling and playing games, they soon discovered that the seventy-four-card deck was too large. Thus, the deck was reduced to fifty-two, symbolic of the number of weeks in a year. Four suits were created (hearts, diamonds, spades, and clubs), to represent the four seasons.

The first face cards came into being in the year 1450. The king was the highest of the face cards, followed by the queen. Next came the jack, symbolic servant to the royal couple.

During the French Revolution in the eighteenth century the king was overthrown. With the royal family gone from real life, some people thought that royalty should also be removed from decks of cards. Thus, for some time cardmakers experimented with new types of face cards. Pictures of famous people were tried, as were pictures of gods and goddesses described in Greek myths. But none of the new face cards ever caught on. In time, everyone went back to the old-time royal decks.

Throughout history many strange and interesting decks of playing cards have been created. There have been silver cards, leather cards, and even rubber cards—for playing games in the bathtub or swimming pool. Square, oblong, and even round cards have been produced. On the backs of some cards can be found advertisements, hand-painted portraits, and propaganda. There was even once a deck that presented an entire picture-history of England.

The popularity of cards and card playing has grown tremendously since their invention by the Chinese so long ago. In the United States alone, seventy million packs of cards are sold every year. And with just one pack of ordinary cards, literally hundreds of different games can be played.

Frozen Foods

Centuries ago an English queen was out for a walk in the countryside. Suddenly she was attacked by a hawk. A man stepped forward and shot an arrow through the eye of the attacking bird. For his deed, the man was given the name "Birds Eye."

Birds Eye is an unusual name with an interesting story behind it. But the name never would have become well-known had it not been for Clarence Birdseye, a descendant of the original Birds Eye.

Clarence Birdseye was an explorer and inventor. In 1916 he went on a wildlife expedition to Labrador. Because he was able to get fresh vegetables only when the supply ship arrived, Birdseye tried to think of some way of preserving them for long periods of time. After a while he hit upon the idea of preserving vegetables in barrels filled with freezing water.

When he returned to the United States, Birdseye started a frozen foods company. The company thrived, and within a few years manufacturers around the world were starting their own companies. Soon not only vegetables but frozen foods of all kinds were appearing in markets everywhere.

Eyeglasses

The story of eyeglasses begins with Nero, who was the emperor of Rome from A.D. 54 to A.D. 68. Of all the Roman emperors, Nero was probably the strangest: he dressed his horses in human clothes; he wandered through city streets at night, singing and dancing; he watched performances by holding a curved, colored jewel in front of one eye.

Though it is not known for sure, it is believed that Nero was nearsighted. Holding a jewel to his eye not only made things prettier, it also helped the funny little emperor see better.

The Chinese were probably the first people on earth to wear glasses at all like those of today. Usually the glasses consisted of two very large oval lenses of rock crystal. The frames were made from the shell of the tortoise. Keeping the glasses in place were two weighted cords that hung over the ears. Or, the glasses were sometimes fastened into hats or had brass bows which clamped against the temples.

Those early Chinese glasses, however, were not an aid to eyesight. People wore them either because they thought it would bring good luck or because they thought it made them look more attractive and important. Often just the empty frames were worn.

Eyeglasses began to appear in Europe around the thirteenth century. Like the Chinese glasses, the lenses were made of rock crystal or some other transparent stone. Europeans, however, did not wear their glasses either for luck or for the sake of appearance: their goal was to improve vision.

The earliest European glasses were merely magnifying lenses, held in the hand. Later came double lenses, framed and held by a handle before the eyes. Next, the handle was done away with; it was replaced by ribbons or strings for tying the glasses to the head. For a while spring-loaded glasses were tried—glasses that clipped onto the nose by a clothespin-like device. Last, but certainly not least, came the idea of using hard wire strands with curved ends for looping over the ears.

Toward the end of the thirteenth century it was discovered that lenses of ground glass were superior to lenses made of clear stone. It is not known for sure, but it is believed that a glazier—a maker of windows—was the first person to manufacture glasses with lenses of this type.

In Europe, for many years after their invention, doctors ridiculed eyeglasses. Most doctors thought that they were dangerous. They said that poor eyesight should be treated with ointments and lotions; wearing glasses would only damage the eyes further.

Obviously, people didn't listen to their doctors. One reason was the growing importance of reading at that time. Each year, more and more people were learning to read. And because glasses—and not ointments—made it possible for the weak-sighted to read, the invention steadily grew in popularity.

Credit for the perfection of glass lenses to improve vision has to be given to America. In 1784 Benjamin Franklin invented bifocals. Though no bigger than dimes, these lenses pointed the way toward ever-greater advances in corrective-lens making.

The first contact lenses were invented in 1877 in Germany. Interestingly, they were not designed to improve vision. They were invented by a scientist whose aim was to protect the eyeball of an individual with a diseased lid.

Chewing Gum

Believe it or not, people have been chewing gum for centuries. The Mayans and other Central Americans chewed chicle, a hardened juice that comes from the sapodilla tree. The people of Asia and Africa chewed wads of grass, leaves, or tree sap for relaxation and enjoyment. The Indians of North America were fond of spruce resin, a chewy substance found in local trees.

When the colonists came to America, they were surprised to see the Indians chewing gum. At first the colonists made fun of the Indians, and thought the habit of chomping on wads of sap was strange and silly. In time, however, the colonists tried the stuff themselves, realized what they had been missing, and were soon out-chewing and out-chomping the native Americans.

In the early 1800s the first shop for making and selling chewing gum came into being. The shop sold pine gum—the same stuff the Indians had been getting for free for hundreds of years.

Soon, more gum shops and factories began popping up. Most of these produced spruce gum; others offered a type of gum made from paraffin.

The kind of gum that people around the world chew today is not made from spruce resin or paraffin. It is made from chicle, the tree juice known to the people of Central America for centuries.

In the year 1870 a photographer by the name of Charles Adams was experimenting with chicle as a substitute for rubber. Adams wanted to make goods such as toys, masks, and rain boots out of chicle, but every experiment failed. Sitting in his workshop one day, tired and discouraged, he popped a piece of his surplus stock into his mouth. As he sat chewing away, the idea suddenly came to him to add flavoring to the chicle and sell it as gum. Twenty years later Adams was a rich man, the owner and manager of a giant chewing-gum factory.

Gum caught on quickly with the American people. Many doctors of the time, however, decided that the rubbery stuff was dangerous to health. For example, in 1869 one physician wrote an article warning that the chewing of gum "would exhaust the salivary glands and cause the intestines to stick together."

In spite of such warnings, the use of chewing gum in the United States has increased rapidly over the years. For example, in 1914 the average American chewed thirty-nine sticks a year; at present the number is almost two hundred sticks a year, and is still on the rise.

According to some psychologists, one reason people chew more gum today is that they are more nervous than the people of the past. One basis for this claim is that every time a war breaks out (something which, quite naturally, makes people very nervous), gum sales around the world immediately skyrocket.

As you can see in any drugstore or supermarket, the production of chewing gum has kept right in step with the ever-growing demand. One estimate has it that almost twenty-four million miles of chewing gum roll out of U.S. factories every year.

The Fork

Forks are funny things: more than a thousand years passed between the time they were first invented and the time people began eating with them.

The first forks were put to many uses, but eating was not one of them. It is known, for example, that ancient people used big wooden forks for farming. They used small, sharp-pointed forks for fishing. They even took their forks to war: the English had a vicious weapon called a fork which had prongs covered with little hooks.

The people of the Middle East were the first to come up with the idea of eating with a fork. Not until the eleventh century did the idea spread to Europe. At that time a woman from Constantinople married a man in Italy. When the woman moved to her husband's homeland she brought a little two-pronged fork with her. Instead of eating with her fingers as everyone else did, she cut her meat in little pieces and ate it with her fork.

The first table fork on record in England is one that belonged to King Edward I in the late thirteenth century. It was made of glass and was considered a great treasure.

By the fifteenth century, the custom of eating with a fork was widespread in many parts of Europe. Of all Europeans, it was the English who resisted this custom the longest. Instead of a fork, the English used a pair of knives to eat their meat. One was for cutting, the other for spearing the pieces.

Not until the seventeenth century did the use of forks become general throughout the western world. By that time even the English had started using the things.

Soap

Primitive people used to bathe in a rather strange way.
First they scoured themselves with a mixture of ashes and
water, which was followed by an application of oil or
grease. Lastly, they rinsed themselves with clean water.

This ancient method of bathing may seem to bear no
resemblance to how we wash today. But the fact is, the
chemical combination of ashes and grease is very similar
to the chemical composition of modern soap. Thus, people
who washed in that way were probably quite successful in
getting themselves clean.

The Sumerians, an ancient people of Babylonia, are believed to have been the first people to make soap. Into a pot of boiling water they would throw ashes and grease. After stirring for a time, they would add salt and a curd would form at the top. This curd was the soap.

Early soap was soft and crumbly. In time, it was learned that a purer, harder soap could be made by washing the curds with a salt solution. Left to settle, the curds would form a hard upper layer of pure soap. This was cut into blocks and made ready for use.

An odd sidelight to our story is the fact that soap is sometimes created accidentally in nature. For example, quite a number of plants and trees contain soaplike substances, substances that both lather and cleanse. Native Americans, as well as other peoples, once used such plants for washing and bathing.

33

Stranger yet is the island of Cimolus, in the Aegean Sea. Incredibly, almost the entire island is made of a greasy soaplike substance. Not only do the inhabitants bathe and launder their clothes with the substance, but when it rains the island is covered with soapsuds to a depth of several feet.

The last type of "natural soap" is rather gruesome—and certainly not suitable for bathing and cleaning. Nonetheless, the fact is that under the proper conditions of moisture and heat, a buried body will turn to soap. Called "grave wax" by undertakers, this strange substance is a chemical much like baking soda mixed with grease, and thus is almost identical in composition to soap. For many years the corpse of William von Ellenbogen, a soldier whose body had turned to soap after he was killed in the Revolutionary War, was on display at the Smithsonian Institution.

The Alphabet

Of all the things people have invented, nothing would be easier to take for granted than the alphabet. Nevertheless, few things rival this invention in importance; none is in such constant use.

Our alphabet is based on one invented by the Greeks about three hundred years ago. Before that time various types of picture writing were used. The problem with picture writing, such as the written languages used by the Egyptians and Chinese, was that a different symbol or picture had to be used for each word. Thus, in order to learn how to read and write, a person had to memorize literally thousands of different symbols.

The idea behind the Greek alphabet was to use letters (symbols) that represented sounds instead of whole words. This system was much better, much simpler: someone learning to read and write had to memorize only a handful of letters, not thousands of complicated pictures.

Not only is our alphabet based upon that used by the Greeks, but our word "alphabet" was made by combining the first two Greek letters—alpha and beta.

Since its adoption by English-speaking people, the alphabet has gone through many changes. For one thing, the order of the letters is different: the sixth letter of our alphabet, for example, is the letter f; the sixth letter of the Greek alphabet was z.

Another way our alphabet has changed is that it has gotten longer. Strange though it may seem, our alphabet once had only twenty-two letters. The missing letters were k, j, v, and w.

During the Middle Ages the letter k was created as a substitute for the letter c where the "hard" sound of that letter was needed. For example, the word "keen" was spelled "cene" until the letter k entered the alphabet to provide a more exact clue to its pronunciation.

At about the same time, the letter *j* was created out of the letter *i*. This is the reason why *j* follows *i* in the alphabet; these are the only two letters that are dotted.

V and *u* are two other letters that look much alike and stand together in the alphabet. The reason is that *v* was once only another form of *u*. Not until the eighteenth century did people begin to use *v* as a completely separate letter.

The most interesting of our new letters is *w*. At one time this letter was written as a double *v* (*v v*) or a double *u* (*u u*). In time, this idea of a double *u* became the letter *w*.

For the last two hundred years our alphabet has stayed the same. This would not have been the case, however, if Ben Franklin had had his way. In 1768 Franklin proposed a scheme to reform English spelling with a new alphabet. He suggested dropping the letters *c*, *j*, *q*, *w*, *x*, and *y*, and substituting six totally new letters so that every sound in the language could be expressed with one letter.

If Franklin's plan had been adopted, our alphabet would probably have been much improved. Generally, the letters Franklin suggested dropping are the most confusing and awkward to use. For example, the letter *y* is often silent; when it is not silent, it sometimes makes the exact same sound as *e* or *i*.

In distinguishing between strong letters and weak letters, Franklin had a keen eye. This becomes clear if we examine a list of the most used—and most useful—letters of today. In order, the letters we use most are *e*, *t*, *a*, *i*, *s*, *o*, *n*, *h*, and *r*. Notice that none of these letters appears on Franklin's "drop" list.

Of course, the alphabet we use is not the only one in the world. At present there are sixty-five different alphabets, almost half of which are in India. Rotakas, a language spoken in the South Pacific, has the fewest letters in its alphabet: it contains only eleven letters—*a*, *b*, *e*, *g*, *i*, *k*, *o*, *p*, *r*, *t* and *u*. The language with the most letters is Cambodian: incredibly, the alphabet for that language contains seventy-four letters.

In the history of language, there have been at least 250 different alphabets; only about a fourth of these are "alive" today. Exactly what lies in store for the alphabet we use now, no one knows for sure. Perhaps it will get longer—or perhaps it will get shorter—or perhaps it will disappear from the face of the earth altogether. Who can say for sure?

The Zipper

The first zippers were not for use on clothes. In the beginning, the things could only be found on shoes and boots.

To tell the story of the zipper we have to go back to the 1890s, the era of high-button shoes. Such shoes required nimble fingers, buttonhooks, and lots of patience to get them on and off.

Living in these times was a man by the name of Whitcomb Judson. Judson, it so happens, was not a patient man. Footwear that sometimes took as much as fifteen minutes to put on did not appeal to him at all.

Seeking a better fastener for shoes, Judson went to work. In time he came up with a thing he called a "clasp locker and unlocker for shoes." Patented in 1893, the device consisted of two thin metal chains that could be joined together by pulling a slider up between them.

The only problem with Judson's invention was that it didn't work very well. More often than not it jammed, snapped, or opened by itself. Not surprisingly, the fasteners were not a big hit with the public: most people stuck to their good old high-button shoes.

Judson was discouraged, but he wasn't ready to quit. He was convinced that his invention would eventually prove to be a very worthwhile one.

In 1896 Judson teamed up with another man, Colonel Lewis Walker. It was Walker who came up with the idea of using the fasteners on all sorts of things, not just shoes.

By 1910 Judson had designed a new, improved fastener. Called the C-Curity, it sold for thirty-five cents. The C-Curity was not for use on footwear, but on men's trousers and women's skirts.

As the years passed, Judson's invention slowly grew in popularity. New uses for the device were being discovered all the time. The only thing the invention now lacked was a good, catchy name.

One day a businessman happened to be visiting Judson's factory. Judson demonstrated how the fastener worked. "My, that's a zipper!" exclaimed the businessman, using a popular expression of the time.

From that day on, Judson's little invention had a name. And that, as you well know, is a zipper!

The Alarm Clock

The E-Z Wake alarm clock was probably one of the strangest, silliest and, possibly, most dangerous contraptions ever invented. The clock hung from the ceiling. When it was time to wake up, a piece of the clock was released and dropped onto the bed. The one major drawback to the E-Z Wake was that it sometimes knocked people out when it woke them up.

You're probably thinking that the E-Z Wake was the world's first alarm clock. From the description, it sounds like a very poor first effort at putting together something that would, at a later date, prove to be a very useful item. But this is not the case. Believe it or not, the E-Z Wake was patented more than a century after a good, workable alarm clock (like the kind we use today) had already been invented.

The E-Z Wake was patented in 1888. In 1787, 101 years before the coming of the E-Z Wake, a clockmaker by the name of Levi Hutchins decided that he would make a clock that "could sound an alarm." The purpose of the clock was to keep him from oversleeping, a habit that had, on more than one occasion, made him late to his job.

Hutchins completed his alarm clock after only a few days of thinking and tinkering. The clock was large, measuring 29 inches by 14 inches, but it worked.

Unlike most inventors, Hutchins wasn't interested in money. His only ambition was to keep himself from over-sleeping, and he never bothered to patent or mass-produce his alarm clock.

Since Hutchins's time there have been many improvements in alarm clocks. They are smaller, more dependable, and easier to use. Many persons have clock-radios, which allow them to awaken to their favorite music.

All that you know. What you probably don't know is that there are, at the present time, a number of wake-up devices on the market totally unlike the ordinary alarm clock. For example, not long ago an inventor came up with a gadget that awakened sleepers by giving them electric shocks. Almost as unpleasant was a device that made the bed start bouncing when it was time to get up. Most unbelievable of all was the Alarm-O-Bed. This bed, at a pre-set time, sprang up on its side, tossing its startled occupant to the floor.

Most of these contraptions are, as you may have guessed, intended only for people who have an especially hard time waking up. According to the manufacturers, they work quite well. That may be so. But what a way to start the day!

The Safety Pin

The year was 1825. And Walter Hunt, a New York inventor, had a problem: he was in debt for fifteen dollars, but he had no money whatsoever. Somehow, overnight, Hunt had to get the fifteen dollars.

The man to whom Hunt owed the money came up with an idea. Knowing that Hunt was an inventor, he came to him and gave him a piece of wire. He told Hunt that he would pay him four hundred dollars for the rights to anything the inventor could make with it.

Three hours later, Hunt came up with a very small but very useful contraption: the safety pin. For this invention Hunt made four hundred dollars, minus the fifteen-dollar debt. The other man made a fortune.

The story of Walter Hunt and his clever invention is a very strange one. Stranger yet is the fact that Hunt did not actually invent the safety pin—he merely improved it. Though Hunt may not have been aware of it, the safety pin was invented almost four thousand years before he was born! The ancient Greeks, Italians, and Sicilians are all known to have used it.

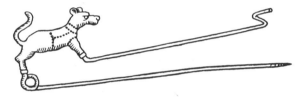

The early safety pin had two things wrong with it. First, it was not safe—the point was not covered, and persons using the thing often got jabbed. Second, the pin had no spring, nothing to hold it firmly in place.

It was Walter Hunt, so many years later, who finally solved these problems. Hunt's pin was safe: when closed, the point was completely concealed. Too, his pin didn't slip: Hunt created a spring for the device by putting a circular twist at the bend.

In later years Hunt went on to invent many things: to name a few, a repeating rifle, an ice plow, and a nail-making machine. Though a brilliant and tireless inventor, Hunt never became a rich man; as with the safety pin, he made little money from any of his creations.

The Postal Service

One day in 1848 a letter arrived for General Zachary Taylor at his home in Baton Rouge, Louisiana. As was common in those days, the letter had no stamp on it. Too, the letter was marked "collect," which meant that the person receiving the letter had to pay for delivery. Annoyed, Taylor refused delivery and had the unopened letter returned to its sender.

Taylor did not know it at the time, but the letter he had sent back unread was probably the most important one he would receive in his life. The letter, as it turns out, informed him that he had been nominated for the presidency of the United States!

Taylor eventually got the news of his nomination. A year later, in 1849, he was elected the twelfth President of the United States.

The story of General Taylor's unopened letter helps to give an idea of how inadequate the postal service was at that time. The fee for handling letters was sometimes paid by the sender, but most often by the receiver. Some letters had crude stamps on them, others bore handwritten symbols, and others had no postal markings at all.

An Englishman by the name of Roland Hill was responsible for reforming the postal system. Hill suggested that letters always be paid for by the sender. He also recommended the use of envelopes with stamps printed directly on them.

Hearing of the proposed reforms, a printer by the name of Chalmers came to Hill and suggested the use of adhesive postage stamps, rather than stamps printed on envelopes.

Hill was excited about the idea. He took a few samples of Chalmers's stamp to the Postmaster-General of England. The stamps, Hill explained, would save time and trouble—and, most important, would put an end to the confusion in the system as it was then.

The Postmaster-General was not impressed. "Of all the wild and visionary schemes I have ever heard of," said the man, "this is the most extravagant."

But in time, Hill was able to persuade the Postmaster-General and the English Government to use his plan. Soon the use of standard adhesive postage stamps had spread worldwide.

The postal service has improved greatly since Hill initiated his reforms more than a century ago. Still, the system is not perfect, and problems and strange mix-ups still occur.

Not long ago a man sent a letter from New York to Canton, Ohio. It arrived three months later, having traveled by way of Canton, *China.*

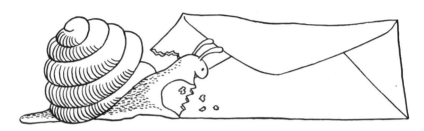

A letter delivered to a man in England had an even stranger fate. Typed on the envelope were the following words: "The Post Office regrets that this cover has been eaten by a snail in the letter box in which the letter was posted."

Last but not least is the story of a man who sent a letter to his sweetheart, asking her to marry him. In his excitement, the man accidentally dropped the letter behind the mailbox instead of into it. For twenty-five years it remained there, until the box was replaced. When discovered, the old and faded letter was, at long last, sent on its way. The woman to whom the letter was addressed accepted the writer's proposal, and the two were married. The bride was then fifty-two, the groom fifty-four. Because of a misplaced letter, the loving couple had lost a quarter of a century of happiness.

The Car

The first car was put on the road in 1863 by a Belgian engineer named Lenoir. The car, which bore his name, looked like a motorized coffin. It had a 1½-horsepower engine and could travel about four miles per hour. Oddly, the contraption was a three-wheeler, having two large wheels in the rear and one small "steer wheel" in the front.

The first person to buy a Lenoir car was Czar Alexander II of Russia. No one knows whether the Czar ever drove the car. In fact, no one knows whether he ever saw it. A short time after it arrived in Russia, the car disappeared without a trace.

Lenoir got the auto industry rolling. However, neither Lenoir nor any other single individual can actually be credited with the invention of the car. In reality, the modern automobile was created over a long period of years by hundreds of different inventors, each of whom made a small but significant contribution. For example, the electric starter was invented in 1896 by an Englishman. Bumpers were invented in 1897 by a Czechoslovakian. Windshield wipers, first introduced in 1916, were the creation of an American.

In 1908 Henry Ford came up with the idea of mass-producing automobiles. Until that time, every car was hand-made by a small team of skilled craftsmen. Realizing that this method was too slow and expensive, Ford designed a conveyor belt that was over one fifth of a mile in length. Down this, the framework of a car slowly moved and parts were added, in carefully controlled order, by a long line of waiting workmen, each of whom had one small job to do.

Because of Ford's invention of the assembly line, automobiles were soon popping up all over America. The era of the horse and buggy was on its way out; the era of the automobile had begun in earnest.

As the automobile began to replace the horse, people thought they saw the coming of a better way of life. Though it sounds incredible to us now, in those days people saw two great advantages to motorized travel: it would be safer and would reduce pollution! "The auto," wrote a newspaper editor in 1911, "will not only be a less hazardous form of travel, it will also put an end to the pollution of our streets caused by the unclean droppings of beasts."

Cars, unfortunately, did not prove to be safer: every year, fifty to sixty thousand Americans die in automobile accidents. And, most certainly, cars did not put an end to pollution: in Los Angeles County alone, they pour more than 10,000 tons of pollutants into the air each day.

Whether we like it or not, our lives today are dominated by the automobile. Believe it or not, the number of cars produced each year in the United States is more than double the number of babies born. To serve all these vehicles, there are presently more than three million miles of highway in this country. Traveling in your car at an average speed of thirty miles per hour, it would take eleven years to cover this distance.

Important as it is to our way of life, the automobile as we know it today is headed for extinction. At its present rate of consumption, this invention will soon burn up what remains of its fuel supply. Either new fuels must be found, or the automobile will disappear forever from the face of the earth.

Paper

Cleopatra, Moses, Julius Caesar, and many other great figures from history never saw a sheet of paper. During the times in which such people lived, writing and drawing were done on slabs of stone, tree bark, papyrus, animal skin, cloth, and just about anything else that could be found.

Not until A.D. 105 did paper come into the world. It was invented by Ts'ai Lun, a Chinese politician. Ts'ai began by taking pieces of old rope, rags, tree bark, and rotted fishnet and letting them soak in a partly filled tub of water. Using a heavy club, he pounded the mixture into pulp, which he poured into a mold. When the pulp had dried, Ts'ai opened the mold and removed the world's first sheet of paper.

For over 500 years the art of papermaking remained in China. Finally, in the seventh century, the art spread to Japan, and from there to the rest of the world.

Until the early 1800s, all paper was made from rags and cloth. Each sheet was made individually, and a good worker could produce about 750 sheets a day.

During the days of rag paper, a bizarre thing happened. A man named Stanwood, a paper manufacturer, found that he was running short of rags. Stanwood's solution to this problem was, to say the least, enterprising: he began importing Egyptian mummies for the sole purpose of un-wrapping them and using the burial cloth to make paper. According to paper historians, the method produced an excellent, heavy brown paper that was sold to grocers for wrapping meat and vegetables. The grisly enterprise, how-ever, came to a sudden halt a few months later when a cholera epidemic broke out among workers assigned to un-wrap the mummies.

Around the middle of the nineteenth century an American by the name of William Tower invented a means of making paper from wood pulp, rather than from rags. Because the new process was easier and more economical, within a short period of time most paper in the world was being made in this way.

The industry expanded rapidly, and paper, which had previously been a rare commodity, soon became abundant, commonplace. A wide range of all sorts of new paper products began to appear on the market. In 1841, the envelope was invented. Nine years later, in 1850, the first paper bags were made. In 1894, automatic machines for making paper boxes came into being.

Today in the United States countless tons of paper are produced every year. Giant machines, some of them more than three stories high, spew out sheets of paper thirty feet wide at speeds up to 2,500 feet per minute.

And what happens to most of this paper? It ends up in the trash! Incredibly, a recent study of American businesses revealed that the average clerk produces 4.4 pounds of waste paper a day. Roughly figured, this means that every clerk in this country throws away the equivalent of a thousand-pound tree every year!

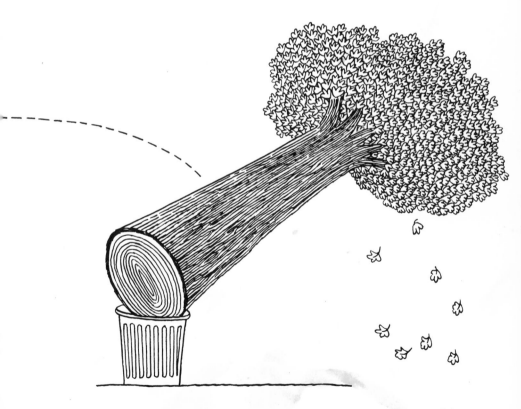

The Bicycle

It is hard to imagine people riding on bicycles in biblical times, yet archaeological finds indicate that they did. Incredibly, bicycles were in existence in Egypt, Babylon, and Italy over two thousand years ago. Those early bicycles could be moved only by pushing with the feet against the ground, and there was no way to steer them.

In 1816 a Frenchman by the name of Niepce invented a bicycle that could be steered. Called a "celeripede," the contraption, including its wheels, was made of wood.

The first really ridable bicycle was made in 1839 by Kirkpatrick MacMillan of Scotland. Dubbed the "hobby-horse" by its inventor, the device could be moved without the rider's feet touching the ground: a pair of cranks connected by rods to the rear wheels were pushed with the feet to make the vehicle go.

In 1871 an Englishman by the name of James Starley invented what would eventually come to be known as the "ordinary" bicycle. This bicycle had a huge front wheel with pedals fitted directly into the hub. As can be imagined, the ordinary was a very unsteady contraption: any attempt at braking, particularly downhill, could send the rider over the handlebars, and a few tumbles were an accepted part of a day's ride.

In 1874 H. J. Lawson designed what he called a "safety" bicycle. Chain-driven, and made with wheels of equal size, the safety was the forerunner to the modern bicycle.

As with every other invention, people have frequently experimented with the design and construction of bicycles, sometimes with rather peculiar results. For example, the longest one ever made was a tandem bicycle that seated ten people. The machine was 23 feet long and weighed 305 pounds.

Another unusual bicycle was one given to actress Lillian Russell by "Diamond Jim" Brady. The bicycle, which cost $10,000, was gold-plated, had mother-of-pearl handlebars, and spokes encrusted with diamonds, emeralds, rubies, and sapphires.

Many strange and interesting feats have been performed on bicycles. For example, a man named Thomas Stevens actually rode around the world on a bicycle. Leaving San Francisco in April of 1884, Stevens pedaled across the United States on his bike, sailed to Europe, resumed his

bicycle travel across Europe and Asia, and sailed across the Pacific, arriving back in San Francisco less than three years after he had set off.

Many persons have traveled across the United States on a bike. The youngest cyclist to achieve this feat was Becky Gorton, age eleven, who arrived at Boston, Massachusetts, on July 22, 1973, having set out from Olympia, Washington, on June 6 of that year.

The highest speed ever achieved on a bicycle was 140 m.p.h. The record was set by Dr. Allan Abbott of San Bernadino, California, pedaling behind a giant windshield mounted on a speeding car.

In addition to a record for going the fastest on a bicycle, there is also a record for going the slowest. This record was set in 1965 by T. Mitsuishi of Tokyo, Japan. Mr. Mitsuishi rode a bicycle for five hours and 25 minutes *without moving*. His overall speed, an electrifying 0 m.p.h., was achieved by simply balancing on the bike while pumping the pedals backward and forward.

The Pencil

One of the strangest things about the lead pencil is that it contains no lead. Rather than lead, the core of a pencil consists of a mixture of clay and graphite.

To understand where the term "lead pencil" comes from, we have to go back to England during the Middle Ages. More precisely, we have to go back to the year 1564.

One winter day in that year, a severe storm toppled a
huge oak tree. When the tree fell, a large deposit of a
strange black substance was revealed. Examining the substance, the local farmers concluded that it was a form of
lead.

In time, the farmers discovered that this unique type of
"lead" was an excellent substance for writing and drawing. They began mining the stuff, digging a huge hole in
the ground at the spot where the oak tree had fallen.

In 1779, more than two hundred years later, an English scientist discovered that the substance coming from the mine was a type of carbon, not lead. Borrowing from the Greek word *graphein*, meaning "to write," he dubbed the substance "graphite," the name by which it is known today.

The first pencils were simply chunks and splinters of graphite. Later, shaped sticks of the material were wrapped with string that could be unwound from one end as needed. Next came tubes of leather or wood into which pieces were pushed, shortly followed by metal holders with clawlike ends for holding the graphite in place.

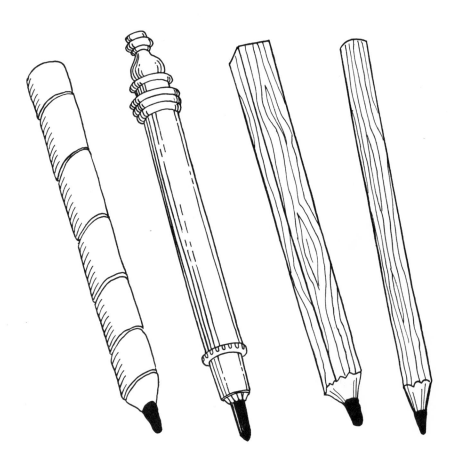

Wooden pencils came into being in 1683. In that year a man named J. Pettus took a small stick of cedar, slit it down the middle, hollowed out the center, inserted a piece of graphite, then glued the whole thing together to create a "wooden" pencil.

For a very long time all wooden pencils were square in shape. Rounded pencils were invented in 1876, by an American named Joseph Dixon.

The first factory for making pencils was built in 1761 in Nuremberg, Germany, by a man named Kaspar Faber. Among Kaspar's many great-grandchildren was a young man by the name of Eberhard. In the year 1848 Eberhard decided to leave Germany and live in the United States. Continuing a family tradition, in 1861 Eberhard built his own pencil factory—the first factory of its kind in America.

Naturally, as soon as people started using pencils, they started making mistakes. And to get rid of their mistakes they needed erasers—the first of which, oddly enough, were edible. The first erasers were nothing but pieces of bread!

Though not very effective, bread lasted for almost two centuries as the world's only type of eraser. Not until 1752 did the rubber eraser come into being, the invention of a Frenchman by the name of Magellan. A few years later an American named Lipman appeared on the scene. And Lipman really topped things off—it was he who came up with the clever little idea of putting the eraser where it really belongs, on the end of the pencil.

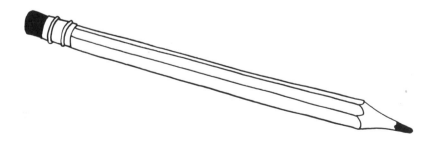

The Rubber Band

The Indians of Central and South America were the first people to make things out of rubber. Using the sap from rubber trees (which abounded in that part of the world), they made rubber coats and hats and toys and skirts.

They even made rubber bottles. And one day in the year 1820, an Englishman named Thomas Hancock was given one of these crude bottles. Taking a knife, he sliced the bottle up into a bunch of rings—and just like that became the inventor of the rubber band.

Hancock turned these first rubber bands into garters and waistbands. Oddly, he never bothered to take out a patent on his invention, and he never realized that rubber bands might be used to do something other than hold up clothes.

Stephen Perry, another Englishman, was the first person to realize that rubber bands could be put to a wide variety of different uses. In 1845 he took out a patent on this invention, and before the year was out had opened up the world's first rubber-band factory.

The Vacuum Cleaner

The first vacuum cleaners blew air out instead of sucking it in. The machines created big clouds of dust, but they didn't get anything clean.

In time, inventors began coming out with cleaners that sucked air in instead of blowing it out. The new machines were better, but they still left a lot to be desired.

For one thing, they had no motors. Suction was created by turning a hand crank or pumping on a foot pedal. Usually two people were needed to operate the machine. One person held the hose; the other turned the crank or pumped the pedal.

Another problem with those machines was that they had no filter. Dust and dirt and crumbs were sucked into a wooden box—and often just blew right back out again.

One day in 1901 a man named Hubert Booth happened to attend a demonstration of a "new model" vacuum cleaner. Booth was not very impressed. He realized that the machines needed to have some sort of filter in them to trap the dust.

At his home that night, Booth had an idea. He took out a handkerchief and laid it on a dusty carpet. Then he put his mouth to the handkerchief and sucked hard. Removing

the handkerchief, he saw that a black circle had formed. The experiment showed that cloth could be used to make an effective filter for vacuum cleaners.

Booth was soon hard at work building a vacuum cleaner. Instead of cranks or pedals, Booth used a gas motor to power his machine. Bag-like cloth filters collected the dust and dirt.

Booth's vacuum worked very well. The only problem with the machine was its size. It was a huge thing, and weighed several hundred pounds!

Because it was so big, Booth decided not to try to sell his invention. Instead, he started a cleaning service. The

vacuum was mounted on a horse-drawn van which brought it to the customer's door. The dust was then sucked out of carpets and furnishings through 800-foot-long hoses which passed through first-floor windows.

Within a few years smaller, portable vacuum cleaners were being built. In 1905 a company in San Francisco put out a 92-pound model mounted on a trolley. Two years later a janitor in Ohio, using a broom handle and a pillowcase, invented the first upright vacuum. In 1908 a man named Hoover went into the business and, within no time, vacuum cleaners were finding their way into houses around the world.

Books

The first books were written by hand, either by skilled slaves or paid professionals. Flourishing publishing industries were in operation in ancient Egypt, Rome, and Greece.

Those early books were papyrus rolls. The rolls dealt with ancient literature, religion, and law, and were purchased by interested citizens in much the same manner that we buy books today.

Books in the form familiar to all of us—made up of pages bound together at one side—came into being around the second century. The earliest were done on parchment by Christian writers of the later Roman Empire. It was in Ireland, however, two or three centuries later, that such books truly became popular.

The early bound book was called a codex, and usually dealt with religious matters. Codices were written entirely by hand by monks, and often took years to complete.

Oddly, there was no punctuation or any spacing between the words in those early books. As with the sixth-century manuscript below, everything was run together.

IGNAROSQVIAEMECVMMISERATVSAGRESTIS
INGREDEREETVOTISIAMNVNCADSVESCEVOCARI
VERENOVOGELIDVSCANISCVMMONTIB·VMOR
LIQVITVRETZEPHYROPVTRISSEGLAEBRESOLVIr
DEPRSSOINCIPIATIAMTVMMIHITAVRVSARATro
INGEMEREETSVCOADTRITVSSPLENDESCEREVOmer

Not until the invention of printing from movable type was it possible to produce books in great quantities. Though the first such book was the *Diamond of Sutra*, published in Korea in 1409, modern printing did not really get its start until 1456, when Johann Gutenberg of Germany printed full-length editions of the Bible. Interestingly, not only was the Bible the first major work ever printed—it is now, and has been for centuries, the number one best-selling book in the world.

The first paperback books were published in 1841. Though printed in Germany, the books were in English and were intended for sale to British and American tourists. Oddly, upon buying a paperback, the purchaser had to agree that he or she would throw it away when finished! Clearly, what the publisher had in mind was the creation of the disposable book—a concept which, in many respects, still underlies the manufacture of paperbacks today.

Throughout history there have been some extremely strange books written. For example, the Japanese Emperor Sutoku (1124–1164) wrote a book *in his own blood!* While in exile for a three-year period, he passed the time by copying the *Lankavara Sutra,* a famous religious essay, using his blood as ink. The work consisted of 135 pages, 1,215 lines, and 10,500 words.

Another oddball writer was a French printer and novelist by the name of Nicolas Bretonne (1734–1806). During his lifetime Bretonne authored 203 books, 152 of which *were never written.* Instead of writing the books, Bretonne simply set the type for them, making up the stories as he went along.

British author E. V. Wright did not typeset his books as he wrote them. Quite the contrary, he labored long and hard with pen and paper in creating the one and only book for which he is known, a novel entitled *Gadsby.* The novel, which contains over 50,000 words, must have been quite an undertaking: *not one word in the book contains the letter* e. As *e* is the most often used letter in the English language, it is difficult to write even one *e*-less sentence, let alone an *e*-less book!

Last but not least in the world of unusual books was one entitled *The Exploits of The Duke d'Épernon*. Published by an enemy of the Duke, the book contains 500 pages, *all of them blank!* The author of the book, without writing a word, made it quite clear to his readers that the Duke d'Épernon had never done anything in his life worth reading about.

Today, vast numbers of new books are published each year—about 40,000 in the United States alone. Some are very good, and some are very bad. And a few are in a class all by themselves—neither good nor bad, they're simply very, very strange.

Traffic Lights

Impossible though it may seem, the traffic light was invented before the car. The first one was installed at a busy intersection in London, England, in 1868, and its purpose was to keep pedestrians from being trampled by horses.

Created by a railroad engineer, the device looked like a railway signal of the time. It had semaphore arms for daytime use, and red and green lamps illuminated by gas for night use. Red indicated "stop"; green indicated "caution." The lantern was turned by means of a lever at the base of the standard so that the appropriate light faced the oncoming traffic.

This first traffic light did more harm than good. After a short period of use, it blew up and killed the policeman operating the lever. After that accident the light was removed, and there were no similar experiments for half a century.

Not until 1914, after the advent of the automobile, did the traffic light reappear. Installed in Cleveland, Ohio, at the intersection of Euclid Avenue and E. 105th St., the signal had only two lights—red for "stop" and green for "go." The first three-color light made its appearance in New York City in 1918.

The early lights were operated manually, usually by a policeman up in a "crow's-nest" lookout tower in the middle of the street. Not until 1926 did automatic signals like those we have today come into being.

Money

It may seem strange today, but food was used as the first money. Salt, essential in early cultures as a preservative, was widely used as a medium of exchange. Pepper, a rather rare commodity until recent times, was next in popularity. Of all the different types of food-money ever in service, the strangest was yak butter: this unlikely currency was used by the ancient people of Tibet, and remains in use in many parts of that country today!

A wide range of objects followed food as money. The people of Egypt used hoes; Fiji Islanders used whale teeth; Africans used iron bars and rods.

About 2700 years ago the first metal coins came into being. Little by little, the idea began to spread around the world.

The Roman coin at the right dates from 44 B.C. The face on the coin is that of Julius Caesar, who died in the same year.

This coin is one of the first ever made in England. It is almost two thousand years old.

This Japanese coin is in the shape of a rectangle. It dates from the year 1837.

The story behind our American coins is a fascinating one. Originally, a penny in this country was worth only half a cent. The coin proved unsatisfactory, so it was decided to make a penny that was worth one cent. The word "cent" comes from the Latin for "hundred," and it takes a hundred pennies to make one dollar.

Only the United States has a coin called a dime. The word comes from medieval times when people paid ten per cent (or, ten per hundred) of their income to the church. This payment was called a "dyme." In 1792 the American Congress decided to create a coin worth ten per cent of a dollar; recalling the dyme of long ago, they decided to call the new coin a dime.

The nickel is another strange coin: until 1866 it was called a "half-dime," and was made of silver, not nickel. But today, now that we have nickels instead of half-dimes, our nickels are still not made out of nickel—they're made from a complex mixture of all sorts of other metals.

One of the most valuable of U.S. coins was a fifty-dollar gold piece issued in the year 1853. Shown below is the only remaining specimen in the world today.

Paper money is believed to have gotten its start in China about 2600 B.C. Printed in blue ink on paper made from the fiber of the mulberry tree, notes nearly 5,000 years old are still preserved.

In addition to inventing paper money, the Chinese also issued both the largest and smallest bill ever printed. In 1368 they issued a *kwan* note which measured 9 inches by 13 inches. Later, they put out a five-cent note which was 2.16 inches by 1.18 inches.

Today we have a new kind of money: credit cards. Though credit cards were invented around the time of World War I, they did not become really popular until the early 1960s.

At present, credit cards are being produced in this country about as fast as money is printed. In fact, some economists predict that it will not be long before we buy everything with credit cards. If this happens, money will become a thing of the past—something to read about in history books and look at in museums.

The Toothbrush

Around the year 1770, a man named William Addis was serving time in an English prison. Sometimes his thoughts would turn to finding a new way of making a living once his term was served.

One morning Addis was cleaning his teeth in the way that people had for centuries: he rubbed them with a rag. Suddenly he had an idea. He found a small piece of bone and bored tiny holes at one end. From the guard he got some brush bristles. He cut the bristles down, wedged them through the holes, and glued them in place. And just like that, the world had its first toothbrush.

When he was released from prison, Addis went into the toothbrush-manufacturing business. The business was an immediate success.

Television

Television is the most popular form of entertainment in the United States today. According to one estimate, the average American spends nine years of his life watching television.

To understand how this amazing contraption came to be, we have to go back to the year 1862. In that year an Italian-born priest, the Abbé Caselli, invented a method of sending pictures over telegraph lines. Caselli's idea was to send drawings and hand-written messages from one place to another. Unfortunately, the pictures Caselli transmitted came out as shadows sprinkled with dots and dashes. Nevertheless, this little-known man should be given credit for being the first person to conceive of anything even remotely resembling modern television.

After Caselli, many inventors around the world tried to put together a device for transmitting pictures. One of these was John Baird, an Englishman.

The year 1924 found Baird hard at work on something he called a televisor. The apparatus consisted of a tea chest, an empty biscuit box, darning needles, an old electric motor, and the lens from a bicycle light. Incredibly, it was this strange collection of odds and ends that would eventually become the world's first workable television set.

In February of 1924, Baird succeeded in transmitting a shadowy picture of a cross onto his "televisor" screen. Though the distance from the camera to the screen was only ten feet, Baird had achieved what, until then, most people had considered impossible.

After an explosion destroyed his laboratory, Baird continued his experiments in a tiny attic workroom. There, in October of 1925, he made his greatest breakthrough. Placing a dummy in front of the camera, the inventor began tinkering and fiddling with his receiver, trying to get it to work. Suddenly the dummy's head appeared on the screen.

Thrilled with his success, Baird rushed downstairs in search of a live subject. The first person he encountered was a fifteen-year-old boy, William Taynton, whom he hustled up to his workshop.

"I placed him before the transmitter," wrote Baird, "and went into the next room to see what the screen would show. The screen was entirely blank. Puzzled and disappointed, I went back to the transmitter, and there the cause of the failure became evident. The boy, scared by the strong light, had backed away from the transmitter. I gave him some

money, and this time he kept his head in the right position. Going again into the next room, I saw his head on the screen quite clearly. It is amusing that the first person in the world to be seen by television needed to be bribed to accept that distinction!"

In the years that followed, great advances were made in television manufacture and technology. By 1931 there were an estimated 30,000 television sets in the United States alone. Prices ranged from $80 to $160 for ready-made sets; construction kits for home-made TVs were available at a price of $36.

In 1941 CBS conducted an experimental color television broadcast. Ten years later, in 1951, regular color transmission began with the airing of *The Ed Sullivan Show,* "Live and in Color."

Almost every year the makers of television sets come up with new additions, innovations, and improvements. For example, today we have video monitoring of the functions of hospital patients, and video monitors used in security systems. There are video recorders, machines that tape-record television shows even while the set is turned off! And there are giant, room-size screens that can make your own home seem like a private movie theater.

Clever as these innovations are, there is more—much more—to come. According to experts, within the next twenty years or so we will see television turned into something beyond our wildest imaginings.

Already, scientists are working on a "new" way of transmitting television signals. Instead of electricity, the television of the future will be powered by light beams— beams that travel not through wire, but through flexible glass fibers. Thinner than a human hair, each fiber will carry *hundreds* of different shows.

No longer will there be only a handful of TV channels to choose from. Replacing the selection knob will be something that looks like a pocket computer. To see the show of your choice, you will simply punch out a code. Time and date will make no difference: you will be able to see any show you wish on any day and at any time that suits you. Program schedules, like those we have today, will disappear altogether.

Future television will provide more than entertainment: it will also provide limitless information. Any page from any book of interest to you will appear on your screen when you punch out a code. If you wish, push another but-

Future television will provide more than entertainment: it will also provide limitless information. Any page from any book of interest to you will appear on your screen when you punch out a code. If you wish, push another button and out will come a printed copy of the page on the screen.

As if this were not enough, scientists see an even greater variety of uses to which television can be put in the not-too-distant future. For example, they say you will someday use your TV to vote, to pay your bills, and to make reservations at hotels and restaurants. Your set will print and deliver your newspaper, supply you with route maps for a vacation, or provide the recipe for a special dish. And in case of an emergency such as a tornado alert, your television will come on automatically to warn you.

Perhaps all of this sounds crazy and impossible and ridiculous to you. That isn't surprising, because that is exactly how people felt about television—until somebody actually invented it.

ton and out will come a printed copy of the page on the screen.

As if this were not enough, scientists see an even greater variety of uses to which television can be put in the not-too-distant future. For example, they say you will someday use your TV to vote, to pay your bills, and to make reservations at hotels and restaurants. Your set will print and deliver your newspaper, supply you with route maps for a vacation, or provide the recipe for a special dish. And in case of an emergency such as a tornado alert, your television will come on automatically to warn you.

Perhaps all of this sounds crazy and impossible and ridiculous to you. That isn't surprising, because that is exactly how people felt about television—until somebody actually invented it.

Mirrors

There are many mirrors in nature: reflections in a pond, in a polished stone, or in a pair of eyes. The first mirrors were all natural. Then came man—and feeling a constant need to see himself, he invented artificial mirrors.

Since the beginning of time, mirrors, whether man-made or natural, have been considered magical. For example, the Basutos, a people of South Africa, believe that crocodiles can drag a person's reflection underwater and kill it. In ancient China, mirrors were set into the gables of houses so that evil spirits would be reflected away. In Western culture, there is an old myth which says that God gave Adam a mirror in which he could see everything on earth; when Adam died, a frog named Fqts got hold of the mirror and buried it beneath an ancient forgotten town.

Whether thought to be magical or not, mirrors have always held a fascination for people. The ancient Greeks, Romans, Egyptians, and Hebrews had mirrors of polished metal. These were usually disks of bronze, with a brilliant polish on the face. Often, the mirror had a decorated back and a handle.

During the Middle Ages people carried little pocket mirrors made of polished steel or silver. Women tucked the mirrors into their sashes and belts; men wore them in their hats.

Mirrors of glass with a metal backing date from the fifteenth century in Europe, and were made in large quantities in Venice in the sixteenth century. At first, such mirrors consisted of a piece of glass fitted against a piece of polished metal; later, liquid metals were used, which made it possible to combine the glass and backing into a single piece.

Today we have two-way mirrors, and mirrors that magnify. There are mirrored walls, mirrored ceilings, and mirrored doors. But even though we live in a world filled with reflections of ourselves, a recent study revealed that most people spend only about twenty or thirty minutes a day looking at themselves in the mirror.

The Bed

Sleeping is very important. It is so important, experts have found, that a person will die more quickly from a lack of sleep than from a lack of food. In fact, after a sleep delay of only twelve hours, the human body needs up to three weeks to return to normal.

People spend about a third of their lives sleeping. Roughly figured, this means that you spend 121 days of each year asleep. If you live to be seventy, you will spend twenty-three of those years asleep.

Because sleeping is so important, so is the bed. Though it is not a very complicated invention, you'd be very uncomfortable without one.

The first bed was probably nothing more than a pile of
leaves. Then came a stone or wooden bench, with a sack of
straw for a mattress and an animal skin for a cover. In
early European homes, sometimes the bench was hidden
away in a little alcove or tiny room with a curtain across
it. During the Middle Ages, benches were abandoned for
more elaborate frames in which mattresses were set.

In the thirteenth century, canopies began to be hung
over the beds from the ceiling, and gradually people took
up the practice of hanging curtains around all four sides.
Beds were so valuable in those times that often a house-
hold had only one, and if a king or lord went visiting, the
bed went too.

During the third century, a bed of solid silver was made for Heliogabalus, the emperor of Rome. In England, in the sixteenth century, a giant bed called the Great Bed of Ware was built. That bed, which still exists in a museum, was ten by eleven feet—big enough for all the members of a really big family to sleep together. Stranger yet, in the seventeenth century a sickly French politician had a portable bedroom made for himself. Carried by twenty-four bodyguards, the room contained a chair, a table, and a bed. In this way, the sickly man was able to go all over the city without leaving his room, and conduct his business while sitting in bed.

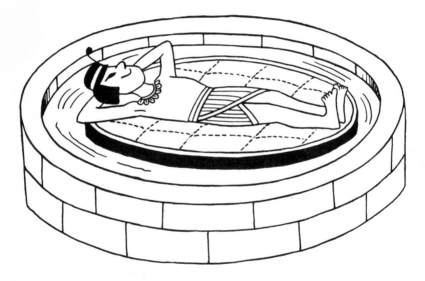

Today's sleep-time oddity is the water bed, something most people probably assume is a rather recent invention. It's not. More than a thousand years ago, Khumarawayn, an Egyptian ruler, slept on an early type of water bed.

The bed consisted of an inflated leather cushion floating on a pool of quicksilver (mercury). According to ancient records, the Egyptian people were quite angry about Khumarawayn's bed. It wasn't that they cared about their leader's weird sleeping habits; they did, however, mind the fact that he levied a special tax on them just to pay for the materials to make the bed.

Today in the United States there are over 200 million beds. They come in every size, shape, and design. We have round beds, motorized beds, water beds, and suspension beds—not to mention lots and lots of plain old ordinary beds. Each of these beds will last an average of fourteen years, which means that most Americans will go through about five in a lifetime.

Truly, the bed is one of the most popular, most used, and most essential of inventions. At the same time, of all inventions, it's the one most taken for granted.

About the Author

Don L. Wulffson teaches English, creative writing, and remedial reading at San Fernando High School in California. He also writes educational books, stories, poems, learning activities, and articles on education. Almost everything he writes for publication he uses in his classroom. A graduate of U.C.L.A., he is the recipient of the Distinguished Achievement Award for Excellence in Educational Journalism given by the Educational Press Association of America (1978). His first book for Lothrop was "Strange, Extraordinary Stories Behind" *How Sports Came to Be*. With his wife and two daughters, he lives in Northridge, California.

About the Artist

Roy Doty is a distinguished illustrator whose work has received many honors. He is the winner of two art director awards, and has been voted Cartoonist Illustrator of the Year three times by the National Cartoonists Society. An author as well as an illustrator, he has had one book published by Lothrop: *Old One-Eye Meets His Match*. A graduate of the Columbus School of Art in Columbus, Ohio, he has been a free-lance artist in the New York area since 1946. With his wife and two of his four children, he lives in West Redding, Connecticut.